A Kid's Guide to
Origami™

Making
ORIGAMI
MASKS
Step by Step

Michael G. LaFosse

The Rosen Publishing Group's
PowerKids Press™
New York

Dedicated to Richard L. Alexander, cofounder of the Origamido Studio

Published in 2004 by The Rosen Publishing Group, Inc.
29 East 21st Street, New York, NY 10010

First Edition

Editor: Jannell Khu
Book Design: Emily Muschinske
Layout Design: Michael J. Caroleo

Photo Credits: All photos by Adriana Skura.

LaFosse, Michael G.
Making origami masks step by step / Michael G. LaFosse.— 1st ed.
     v. cm. — (A kid's guide to origami)
Includes bibliographical references and index.
Contents: What is origami? — Mardi Gras mask — Monster mask — "Mr. Whiskers" cat mask — Skull mask — Daruma — Elf mask — Talking bird mask — Fox mask.
ISBN 0-8239-6703-4 (library binding)
1. Masks—Juvenile literature. 2. Origami—Juvenile literature. [1. Origami. 2. Masks. 3. Paper work. 4. Handicraft.] I. Title. II. Series.

TT898 .L34 2004
736'.982—dc21

                                          2002153459

Manufactured in the United States of America

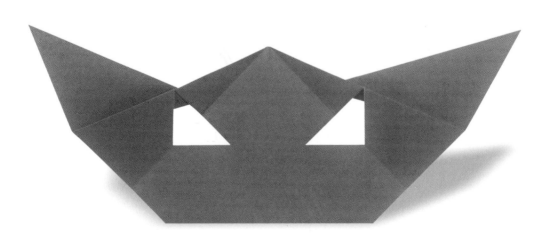

Contents

What Is Origami?

Origami is the art of paper folding to make different shapes. Origami is a Japanese word. *Ori* means "fold" and *kami* means "paper." People throughout the world enjoy folding and inventing new origami shapes. Origami **instructions** are usually shown in drawings, much like the ones in this book. This book also has written instructions under each drawing instruction. Study the origami key at the back of this book on page 22, and you can learn how to make origami from any origami book, no matter what country it is from.

The origami masks in this book are folded from square-shaped paper. Square paper can be made from many kinds of paper, such as gift-wrap paper, printer paper, craft paper, and construction paper. If you are using origami paper, be sure to start with the colored side facedown. Masks can be made small enough to cover only the upper part of your face, or big enough to cover your entire face. The best part of origami is that you can experiment with different shapes and styles.

Although origami objects are made by folding paper, sometimes cutting is necessary. For instance, you may need to use a pair of scissors to cut holes for the eyes. You will enjoy learning how to make these masks. Origami masks are fun to make and fun to wear, and they also make great gifts and decorations.

Mardi Gras Mask

Mardi Gras is French for "fat Tuesday." For some **Christians**, Mardi Gras is the last chance to **celebrate** before Lent. Lent is the period of 40 days before Easter when many Christians give up something they enjoy. Lent ends on Easter Sunday. Many Christians see Lent as a time of **spiritual renewal** and **fasting**.

Mardi Gras is a time of fun, food, and **festivities**! People often dress in costumes and wear masks to parties and parades during Mardi Gras. Perhaps some people enjoy themselves so much that they are afraid to be recognized! This Mardi Gras Mask hides only the upper part of your face. That way, you are free to laugh, smile, talk, and eat.

1

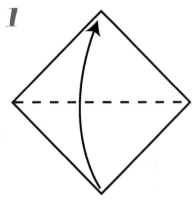

Use an 8-inch- (20.3-cm-) square paper. Valley fold in half, bottom corner to top corner.

2

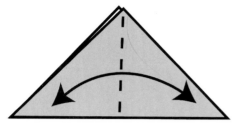

Valley fold the paper in half, from the left corner to the right corner. Unfold the paper.

3

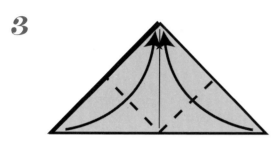

Valley fold up the left and the right corners to match up to the top corner.

4

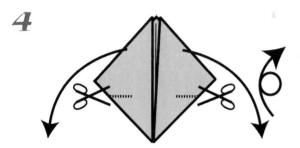

Cut a slit on both the left and the right side of the folded edges. Notice that the cuts are made below the left and the right corners. Unfold the top two corners. Turn the paper upside down.

5

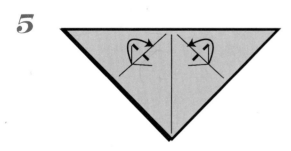

Open the eye holes by folding up the two cut corners.

6

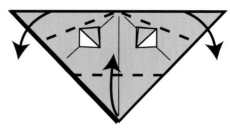

Valley fold up the bottom corner, but not so high as to cover the eyes. Valley fold down the two top corners. Be sure that they make a wide shape.

7

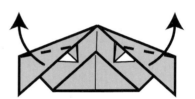

Valley fold up the two corners to make the two horns.

8

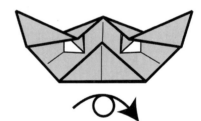

Turn the paper over.

9

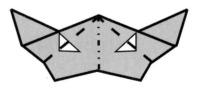

Mountain crease the center of the mask. Valley fold the creases that line up with the eye holes.

Monster Mask

Many monsters look scary because their facial features are out of **proportion**. For instance, some monsters have huge mouths full of sharp, bone-crushing teeth. This origami mask has such teeth. After you make this mask, you can separate its upper and lower jaws. You can also add a long, red, forked tongue to make your mask look even scarier. Experiment with the cuts and folds in the eyes to make your monster look mad, sad, or even happy. Try changing the shape of the horns. When the horns don't stick up, the monster looks less angry.

1

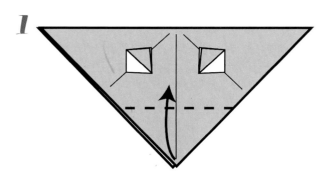

Use an 8-inch- (20.3-cm-) square paper. Go to page 7. Fold the mask up to step 5 and come back to this page. Next valley fold up the bottom corner, but not so high as to cover the eye holes.

2

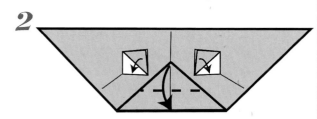

Valley fold down the triangle corner to touch the middle of the bottom edge. Fold down the top layer of each of the eyes.

3

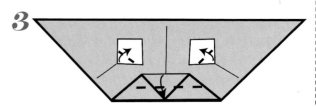

Valley fold down the folded edge to match the bottom edge. Make the pupils by folding up the corner of each of the eye papers.

4

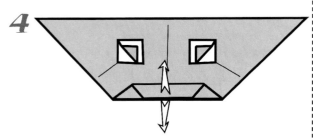

Pull open the paper at the bottom and separate the two layers, one up and one down.

5

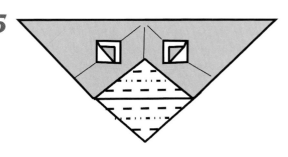

Use the creases to mountain fold and valley fold the triangle papers like a fan. These will become the monster's teeth.

6

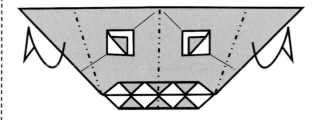

Mountain fold the left and the right corners around the back. Mountain crease the center line.

7

Valley fold the monster's horns in half.

Cat Mask

This origami Cat Mask has wide cheeks, perky ears, and bright whiskers. Whiskers help cats to sense their surroundings. For instance, if a cat is chasing a mouse and the mouse runs inside a narrow passage, the cat's whiskers help it to know if it can fit inside the passage. If the passage is too narrow, the cat could get trapped. You can give your Cat Mask a different look by folding its whiskers down or slitting them with scissors to make them curl. Try changing the angle of the eye cuts to make the Cat Mask look wild or pleasant.

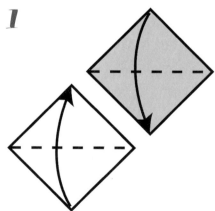

1

Use two 8-inch- (20.3-cm-) square papers. Fold both of them in half, one from the top to the bottom corner, the other from the bottom to the top corner.

2

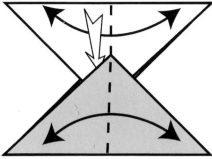

Valley fold each paper in half, corner to corner. Unfold the papers. Slip the top triangle into the bottom one. Line up the two triangles along the center crease line you made.

3

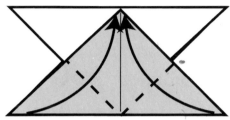

Valley fold up the bottom corners to the middle of the top. Use the center crease line as a guide to do these folds.

4

Cut a curved slit on the left and the right sides of the bottom paper. Unfold the triangle corners and turn the paper upside down.

5

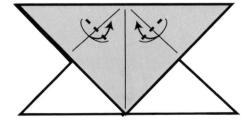

Open the eye holes by folding up both cut paper layers.

6

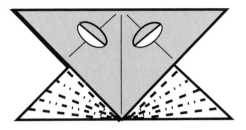

Valley fold and mountain fold the bottom triangle corners, as you would for a fan, to make the cat's whiskers.

7

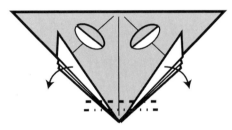

Valley fold and mountain fold the bottom corner to make the nose. Pull out the whiskers.

8

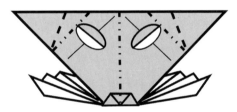

Mountain fold and valley fold the top two corners to make the ears. Mountain fold the center crease.

9

This is how your finished cat mask should look.

Skull Mask

Many countries pay respect to the **deceased**. In Mexico, the Day of the Dead is held on November 1 and 2. It is a time to honor family members who have passed away. It is not a sad time but a joyous one. Families celebrate the Day of the Dead with flowers, food, and parades. Families visit the graves of their **ancestors**. Human **skeletons** and skulls are common **symbols** of this Mexican holiday. Mexicans make candies and pastries formed in these shapes, and they wear or display skull masks. You can use this Skull Mask on the Day of the Dead.

1

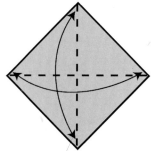

Use a 10-inch- (25.4-cm-) square paper. Fold and unfold from top to bottom and from side to side.

2

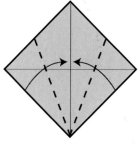

Fold the bottom two edges to meet at the center crease line to make a kite shape.

3

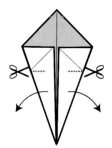

Cut two slits, one on each side, at the level where the creases touch the folded edges of the paper. Unfold the kite shape.

4

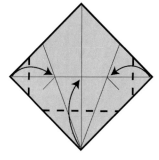

Fold up the bottom corner to touch the center of the paper, where the creases cross. Fold in the left and the right corners to the place where the slits meet the crease line.

5

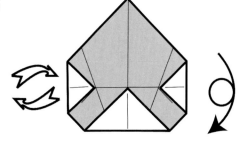

Turn the paper over, and rotate it as shown.

6

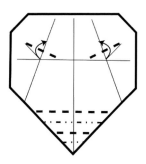

Open the eyes by folding up the cut edges of paper. Mountain and valley fold the bottom corner to make the teeth. This is the same manner in which the teeth were folded for the Monster Mask, on page 9.

7

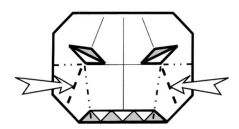

Using the crease marks, mountain and valley fold the sides of the skull to make the jaw narrow. Push in the sides of the skull as shown.

8

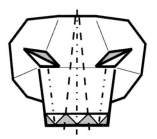

Make the skull mask less flat by adding these mountain folds and valley folds.

Daruma Mask

Daruma was a monk who was born in India. He traveled to Japan to spread his faith, **Buddhism**. Today in Japan, Daruma is often **represented** by a **papier-mâché** doll without **pupils**. The eyes of the Daruma doll are left empty for a reason. When the owner makes a wish, he paints in one of the eyes. When the wish comes true, he paints in the other eye. You too can make a wish with this Daruma Mask. After you fold this origami mask, make a wish and fold over only one eye corner to make the pupil. When your wish comes true, fold up the other corner.

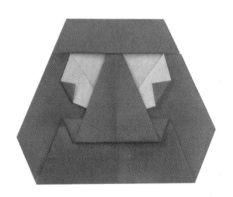

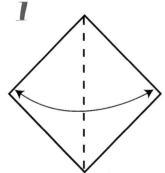

1

Use a 10-inch- (25.4-cm-) square paper. Fold it and unfold it as shown.

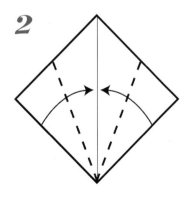

2

Fold the bottom two edges to meet at the center crease to make a kite shape.

3

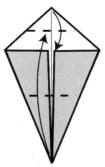

Valley fold down the top corner to the top of the folded corners. Valley fold up the bottom corner to touch the middle of the top folded edge.

4

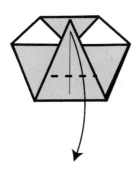

Valley fold down the top corner.

5

Valley fold down the two corners to form the eyes.

6

Valley fold down the top edge to match the level of the top of the eyes. Next fold up the bottom corner to fit just under the flap you folded down earlier in this step.

7

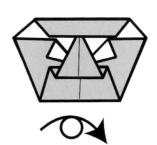

Turn the paper over.

8

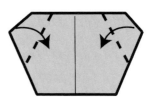

Make the top narrower by folding in the left and the right corners. They should not meet in the middle of the paper.

9

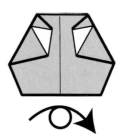

Turn the paper over.

10

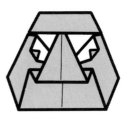

To make wishes using the Daruma Mask, make a wish and fold up one eye corner. When your wish comes true, fold up the other eye corner so that Daruma has both of his eyes. Good luck with your wishes!

Elf Mask

Most people think of elves as funny and playful creatures. Perhaps it is the way they look, with their bright eyes and big ears. There are many kinds of elves. Irish **leprechauns** and the little people who help Santa Claus to make Christmas toys are elves. People believe elves have magical powers. See if you have magical powers when you wear this origami Elf Mask! This Elf Mask also makes a great decoration for St. Patrick's Day or Christmas. Attach a loop of ribbon to make it a hanging ornament, or use it to decorate a greeting card or a gift.

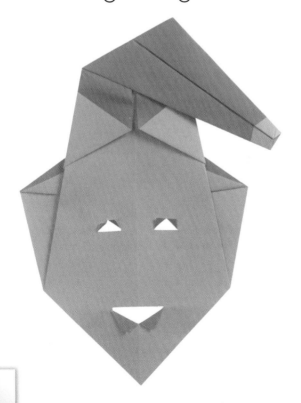

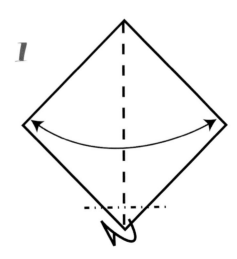

1

Use a 10-inch- (25.4-cm-) square paper. Fold it from left to right and unfold. Mountain fold the bottom corner back to the other side.

2

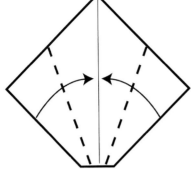

Valley fold the bottom two edges to meet at the center crease line.

3

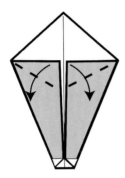

Valley fold the two corners at a slight angle.

4

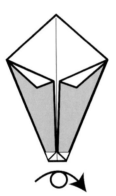

Turn the paper over.

5

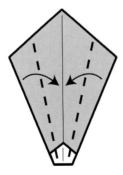

Valley fold the left and the right edges to meet at the center crease line.

6

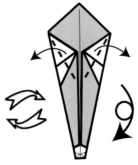

Valley fold the two corners to make the ears. Turn the paper over and flip it upside down.

7

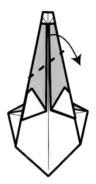

Valley fold down the top of the hat at an angle.

8

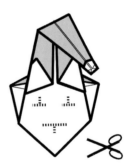

Cut slits in the paper to make a mouth and two eyes. You can draw or paint a face instead if you wish.

9

Fold open the eyes and the mouth.

Bird's Beak Mask

Each kind of bird has its own special kind of beak, depending on what kind of food it eats. A parrot has a short, strong beak that can crack open hard nut shells. A hummingbird's beak is long and thin so that it can reach the sweet **nectar** found inside flowers. Try looking at the shape of a bird's beak and guessing what kind of food it eats! This origami Bird's Beak Mask is easy to fold and fun to wear. If you press each cheek, the beak opens and closes. Try using the beak to pick up a small object, such as a crumpled paper ball.

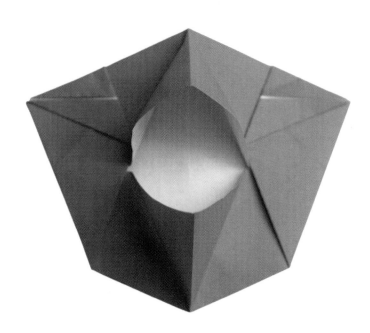

1

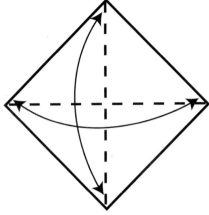

Use a 10-inch- (25.4-cm-) square paper. Valley fold and unfold it in half, corner to corner, both ways.

2

Valley fold the top and the bottom left sides to meet at the center crease line and then unfold.

3

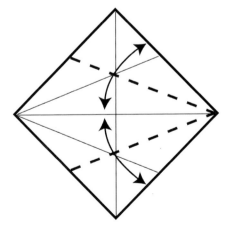

Valley fold the top and the bottom right sides of the paper to meet at the center crease line and then unfold.

4

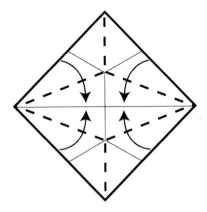

Using all the creases that you made, form the bird's beak by bringing the four edges of the square to meet at the center crease. The top and the bottom corners will fold in half and stick up at the middle of the paper.

5

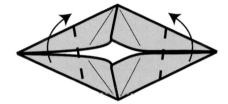

Valley fold the right and the left corners.

6

Valley fold the top corners out to the sides to make the eyes.

7

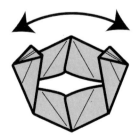

Open and close the beak by folding and unfolding the mask in half.

Fox Mask

If you have seen a fox, you will **appreciate** this Fox Mask. The small eyes, sharp nose, and **alert** ears make this Fox Mask look almost like the real thing. Foxes often hide in bushes and stand still, as if they aren't even breathing, in order to catch mice by surprise. Foxes must use their strong sense of smell and their strong sense of hearing to find enough **prey** to eat. This mask doesn't have eyeholes. It is a different kind of mask that is worn on the top of your head. Wear this mask and get down on your hands and knees to look like a real fox!

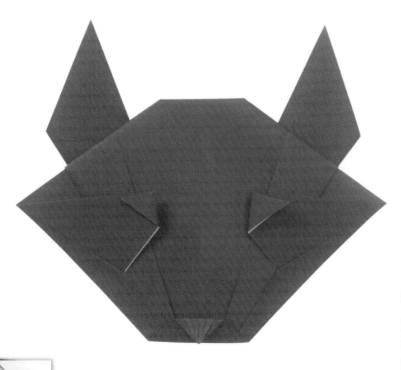

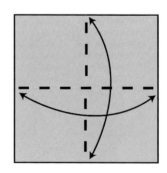

1

Use a 10-inch- (25.4-cm-) square paper. Valley fold and unfold it from top to bottom and from left to right. Turn the paper over.

2

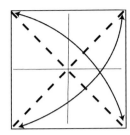

Valley fold the paper in half both ways, corner to corner, unfolding it after each fold.

3

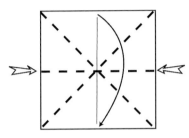

Valley fold the top of the paper down to meet the bottom, while pushing in the sides of the paper. Use the creases that you made in steps 1 and 2 to do this. Look ahead to step 4 to see the shape.

4

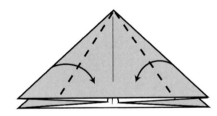

Valley fold the left and the right edges of the top layer. Notice the angle. The edges do not meet at the center crease. Look at step 5 to see the shape. These corners will become the fox's ears.

5

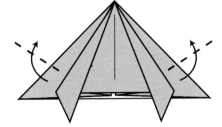

Use the dotted lines to fold up the back corner layers behind the top layers. Look ahead to step 6 and see where the corners should go.

6

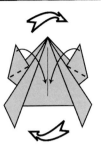

Fold the top corners toward the center of the paper. Rotate the paper from top to bottom.

7

Valley and mountain fold the bottom corner to make the nose. Valley fold the inner tips of the eye paper, one to the left and one to the right.

8

Open the tips of the eye corners. Mountain and valley fold the ears behind the head.

9

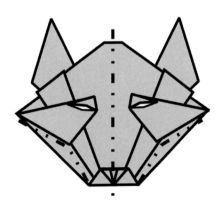

Mountain fold the center crease and the paper edges on the left and the right side of the nose.

Origami Key

1. MOUNTAIN FOLD

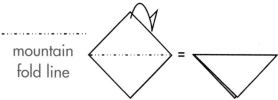

mountain fold line

Notice the mountain fold line. To make a mountain fold, fold the paper back away from you, so that it meets at the other side.

2. VALLEY FOLD

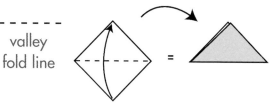

valley fold line

Notice the valley fold line. To make a valley fold, fold the paper toward you.

3. MOVE, PULL, PUSH, SLIP

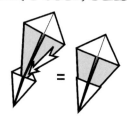

4. DIRECTION ARROW

5. FOLD and UNFOLD

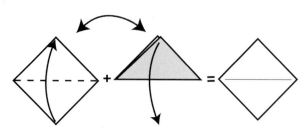

6. TURN OVER

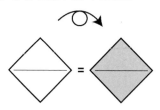

7. ROTATE

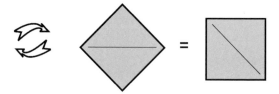

8. CUT

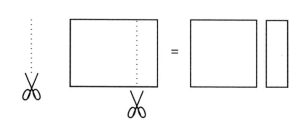

9. REPEAT

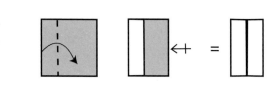

Glossary

alert (uh-LERT) Quick to learn and act.

ancestors (AN-ses-terz) Relatives who lived long ago.

appreciate (uh-PREE-shee-ayt) To understand the value of.

Buddhism (BOO-dih-zum) A faith based on the teachings of Buddha, started in India.

celebrate (SEH-luh-brayt) To observe an important occasion with special activities.

Christians (KRIS-chun) People who follow the teachings of Jesus Christ and the Bible.

deceased (dih-SEESD) Dead.

fasting (FAST-ing) Choosing to go without food.

festivities (fes-TIH-vih-teez) Large parties or gatherings.

instructions (in-STRUK-shunz) Explanations or directions.

leprechauns (LEP-ruh-konz) Elves from Irish fairy tales.

nectar (NEK-tur) A sweet liquid found in flowers.

papier-mâché (pay-per-mah-SHAY) Paper mixed with water to make a paste that can be molded when wet. When it dries, it becomes hard and strong.

prey (PRAY) An animal that is hunted by another animal for food.

proportion (pruh-POR-shun) The measure of one part compared to another.

pupils (PYOO-pulz) The openings in the eyes that change size to let the right amount of light into the eyes.

renewal (reh-NOO-ul) To make new or whole again.

represented (reh-prih-ZENT-ed) Stood for.

skeletons (SKEH-lih-tunz) The bones in an animal's or a person's body.

spiritual (SPEER-ih-choo-ul) Blessed, religious.

symbols (SIM-bulz) Objects or pictures that stand for something else.

Index

Web Sites

Due to the changing nature of Internet links, PowerKids Press has developed an online list of Web sites related to the subject of this book. This site is updated regularly. Please use this link to access the list:
www.powerkidslinks.com/kgo/masks/